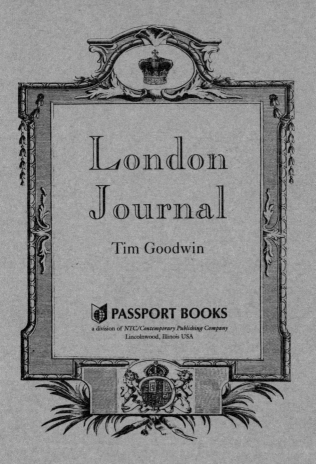

London
Journal

Tim Goodwin

PASSPORT BOOKS

a division of *NTC/Contemporary Publishing Company*
Lincolnwood, Illinois USA

Soveraign of cities, semeliest in sight,
Of high renoun, riches, and royaltie;
Of lordis, barons, and many goodly Knyght;
Of most delectable lusty ladies bright;
Of famous prelatis in habits clericall;
Of merchauntis full of substance and myght:
London, thou art the flour of Cities all.

William Dunbar (1456–1513)

CONTENTS

HISTORIC LONDON

THE BRIDGE

S. Mary Overis

EARLY LONDON
43–1066

Julius Caesar

*L*ondon was founded by invaders from the other side of Europe – the Romans. Julius Cæsar passed this way in 55BC and nearly a century later in 43AD, the Roman emperor Claudius dispatched an army to conquer the troublesome Celts who made the river Thames their main line of defence. The Romans bridged the Thames for the first time and called the settlement Londinium, probably from the original Celtic name. A great fire destroyed part of the city around 125, but it was soon rebuilt and became the fifth largest city north of the Alps. After the Romans withdrew in 410, the city fell into decay. In 540 a monk wrote regretfully that 'the cities of our country are still not inhabited as they were; even today they are squalid, deserted, ruins'. London was taken by the invading Saxons in around 570. The country was split into many different kingdoms for the next three centuries, and not until about 1000 did London again establish itself as the most important city in the country.

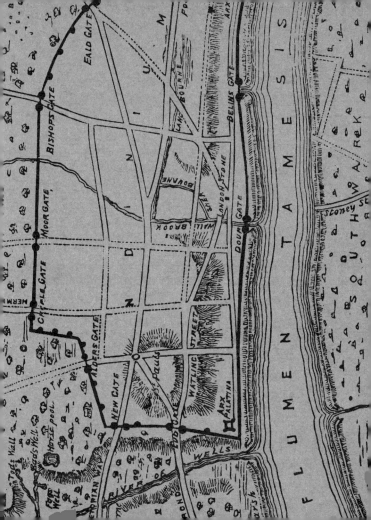

PLANNING NOTES

Roman remains

No parts of Roman Londinium exist above street level. However, many artifacts, including a wall painting and mosaics, can be seen in the **Museum of London**. The remains of a hypocaust – a central heating system – exist beneath Lower Thames Street.

The remains of a temple to the god Mithras can be seen in Queen Victoria Street in the City. The crypt of **All Hallows by the Tower**, Byward Street, has a Roman pavement and crosses, and the Saxon arch in the south-west corner of the church contains Roman tiles. **The London Stone**, set in the wall of 111 Cannon Street, is said to be the milestone from which all measurements in Roman Britain were made.

Around the year 200 a wall was built around Londinium, either to protect it from barbarian attacks or because of civil war among the Roman rulers. A few sections of the Roman wall, as discovered in medieval times, can still be seen in **St Alfege Church** at London Wall; in Wardrobe Tower at the **Tower of London**, Tower Hill; in the **Museum of London** garden and in the underground car park at London Wall.

NOTES

William of
Normandy

MEDIEVAL LONDON
1066–1485

*I*n 1066, William of Normandy (r.1066–87) crossed
the English channel, defeated King Harold at the
Battle of Hastings and marched on London to establish a new
empire, and unite the country under the rule of one monarch.
During his reign trade flourished and the City of London
thrived as a commercial centre with well–organised companies
and guilds and strict urban planning laws. London was by far
the most important city in the kingdom, with a population of
around 50,000. The **Palace of Westminster** became the
centre of English law and government and in 1215 King
John was petitioned by the City merchants to sign the Magna
Carta (great charter) establishing the first democratic
traditions of self-rule. The **Houses of Parliament**, the Lords
and the Commons, were established (at Westminster) in the
14th century. London was granted formal status as a
commune with the privilege of electing a powerful mayor.

FIRST IMPRESSIONS

When I am in a serious humour, I very often walk by myself in Westminster-abbey: where the gloominess of the place, and the use to which it is applied, with the solemnity of the building, and the condition of the people who lie in it, are apt to fill the mind with a kind of melancholy or rather thoughtfulness that is not disagreeable. I yesterday passed a whole afternoon in the church-yard, the cloisters, and the church, amusing myself with the tombstones and inscriptions that I met with in those several regions of the dead. Most of them recorded nothing else of the buried person, but that he was born upon one day, and died upon an other; the whole history of his life being comprehended in those two circumstances that are common to all mankind. I could not but look upon these registers of existence, whether of brass or marble, as a kind of satire upon the departed persons; who had left no other memorial of them, but that they were born, and that they died.

Joseph Addison, *The Spectator*,
30 March 1711

Westminster Abbey

Edward the Confessor began work on **Westminster Abbey** in 1049. The unfinished church was consecrated on 28 December 1065, ten days before Edward died. A year later, on Christmas Day 1066, William the Conqueror was crowned king in the Abbey. His mercenary troops mistook the cheers of the crowd for a riot and set fire to neighbouring houses. The Abbey was rebuilt in the 13th century. All but two of the kings of England have been crowned here. In the Abbey is **Poet's Corner**, the country's most famous burial ground, where lie England's greatest literary figures, including most recently poet John Betjeman.

Westminster Abbey, with its ornate flying buttresses, chapels, carvings, stonework and tapestries, is the place to savour the richness of English history.

Tower of London

William the Conqueror recognised the crucial importance of London, and built the **White Tower**, the oldest part of the Tower of London, to control and protect the fast growing capital. **The Bloody Tower**, originally the Garden Tower, is the place where Richard III (r.1483–5) arguably had his young nephews, Edward V (r.1483) and the Duke of York, murdered. Centuries later skeletons believed to be those of the Princes in the Tower were discovered under a staircase, and were later reburied in **Westminster Abbey**.

Other famous prisoners of the Tower included Richard II (r.1377–99) who signed his abdication here, and Henry VI (r.1422–61) who went mad after being forcibly deposed by Edward IV (r.1461–83). Edward's brother, the Duke of Clarence, was murdered in the Tower in 1478 by being drowned in a butt of Malmsey wine. Sir Thomas More, Henry VIII's chancellor and a saint of the Roman Catholic church, was murdered in the Tower in 1535 for refusing to accept Henry VIII's remarriage. Two of Henry's wives, Anne Boleyn and Catherine Howard, were executed here for infidelity. The famous explorer Sir Walter Raleigh was imprisoned in the Tower for 13 years by King James I and finally executed in 1618 on the request of the Spanish, who hated him for raiding their colonies. The most recent prisoner was Hitler's deputy, Rudolf Hess, who was held in the Tower in 1941 after his flight to England.

The 42 Yeoman Warders, or 'Beefeaters', are known for their scarlet and gold Tudor uniforms, although they are more likely to be seen in dark blue Victorian dress. The company was founded in 1485, to guard the Tower. Today they guide visitors. The name Beefeater is a 17th-century term of abuse intended only for well-fed domestic persons.

Westminster Hall

Westminster Hall was built by William II (r.1087–1100) in 1097. It was used in the Middle Ages for joustings, Christmas feasts and grand ceremonies. It was extensively rebuilt by Richard II in the 14th century, with a remarkable timber roof and fantastic carved flying angels. It is the only surviving part of the **Palace of Westminster**. It was here that Charles I (r.1625–49) was put on trial for his life in January 1649, accused of 'high treason and misdemeanours'. When he was allowed to answer the charge, Charles warned the judges, 'Remember I am your king, your lawful king, and what sins you bring upon your heads, and the judgement of God upon this land; think well upon it.' Subsequently he denied the right of the court to try him, and remained largely silent during the eight days of the trial.

NOTES

Edward II

NOTES

The Guildhall

Even in medieval years, London was turning into a
commercial centre. While it was ruled by the monarchy
London had a unique style of self-government, the
Corporation of London. Councillors, aldermen and a
powerful mayor provided the financial engine to support
London's enormous growth. The seat of this power was
concentrated in the magnificent Guildhall.

Today's Guildhall was begun in 1411 and has, like many of
London's famous edifices, been built and devastated and
rebuilt over the centuries. There are splendid carvings
throughout the halls. The name Guildhall is taken from the
ancient craft and social guilds which formed a large part of
the fabric of London life for hundreds of years.

I was guest at a lunch given in honour of the Lord
Mayor ... In this room, which is called the
Guildhall there were sixteen tables besides others
in the adjoining rooms; in all, nearly 1,200
persons dined, all with the greatest pomp.

Joseph Haydn, letter to Maria Anna von Grenzinger,
1791, from *The Collected Correspondence and London
Notebooks of Joseph Haydn*, H C Robbins, 1959

Dick Whittington

Richard Whittington was the third son of a Gloucestershire country gentleman. At the age of 13 he set out for London, to become one of the City's most prosperous and successful men. He was chosen Lord Mayor of London in 1397, 1398, 1406 and 1418. He died childless and left all his money to charity. Although he is just about the only Lord Mayor of London that anyone can ever remember, his name is more commonly associated with the pantomime character Dick Whittington, who comes to London after hearing that the streets are paved with gold. On Highgate Hill the statue of a black cat, belonging to the fictional Dick Whittington marks the spot where the young Whittington is said to have stopped on his way out of London, and heard the bells of St Mary-le-Bow (Bow Bells) chime 'turn again, Whittington, thrice Mayor of London'.

TUDOR LONDON
1485–1603

Henry VIII

*L*ondon grew explosively under the Tudors. This was a period of rapid commercial growth, when England was spared the destruction and suffering of a century of religious wars which devastated the European mainland. Seafaring adventurers such as Francis Drake and Walter Raleigh established new trade routes, and the English navy confirmed its pre-eminence with the defeat of the Spanish Armada in 1588. The discovery of the Americas and the Turkish conquest of most of the Mediterranean combined to tilt trade towards the Atlantic, to the benefit of the English. The dissolution of the monasteries, following Henry VIII's break with the Roman Catholic church in 1534, placed enormous wealth in private hands and led to a massive property boom. Many palaces were built or transformed in this period, including **St James's**, **Greenwich** and **Hampton Court**. Henry's daughter Elizabeth ushered in a golden age of trade, a period often referred to as 'Merrie England'.

NOTES ON
HISTORIC SITES

St James's Palace

At the end of Pall Mall is St James's Palace, built by Henry
VIII in 1532 on the site of a lepers' hospital. After Whitehall
Palace burnt down in 1698 St James's became the principal
royal residence until 1820. Even after the monarch left,
foreign ambassadors continued to be (and still are) accredited
to the Court of St James's. **Clarence House**, built in 1828
by John Nash (1752–1835), the architect responsible for
redesigning much of London's West End, is part of St
James's Palace and is presently the residence of Queen
Elizabeth, the Queen Mother. The
gatehouse on the south side of St James's
is the only large part of the original
building to survive, the remainder
from Nash's period of influence.
The clock on the gatehouse
is from Tudor times; a
minute hand and a new dial
were added in 1831. St
Jame's is currently the
home of the Duke and
Duchess of Kent, only
Friary Court and the
Chapel Royal are open
to the public.

All the beauty of this island is confined to London; which, although sixty miles distant from the sea, possesses all the advantages to be desired in a maritime town; being situated on the river Thames ... Although this city has no buildings in the Italian style, but of timber or brick like the French, the Londoners live comfortably, and, it appears to me, that there are not fewer inhabitants than at Florence or Rome. It abounds with every article of luxury, as well as with the necessaries of life: but the most remarkable thing in London, is the wonderful quantity of wrought silver ... In one single street, named the Strand, leading to St Paul's, there are fifty-two goldsmith's shops, so rich and full of silver vessels, great and small, that in all the shops in Milan, Rome, Venice, and Florence put together, I do not think there would be found so many of the magnificence that are to be seen in London.

Andrea Trevisan, a Venetian diplomat
in London in 1498, from *Relations or Rather
a True Account of the Island of England*,
ed. C A Sneyd, 1847

The Inns of Court

The Magna Carta of 1215 provided for the Court of Common Pleas to be established in a permanent home at Westminster. As a consequence leading lawyers congregated nearby.

After the order of fighting monks, the Templars, was disbanded in 1312, its property was bought by lawyers, who established the Inns of Court as places of study. The most famous are the **Inner** and **Middle Temple**, **Gray's Inn** and **Lincoln's Inn**.

Temple Church, begun around 1160, is one of four circular churches in England, all of them based on the Church of the Holy Sepulchre in Jerusalem. It contains a penitential cell, too small to lie down inside, where one disobedient member of the order of Templars is said to have been left to starve to death.

Middle Temple Hall was built in 1573. Its roof is probably the best piece of Elizabethan architecture in London. The feasts held in this hall were famous and featured trumpeters, boars' heads, armed men on mules, plays (including one of the first performances of Shakespeare's *Twelfth Night*) and dances. The building was saved from the Great Fire.

Some parts of **Lincoln's Inn** date from the 16th century, notably the 1518 gatehouse. The playwright Ben Jonson is said to have worked there as a bricklayer, 'having a trowel in one hand, he had a book in his pocket'. **Staple Inn**, High Holborn, is behind a façade of 16th-century shops.

Sutton House, Homerton High Street, is a Tudor merchant's house built in 1535.

NOTES

Hampton Court

Hampton Court, a palace in all but name, was built by Cardinal Wolsey in 1514. Wolsey was described by the Venetian ambassador as 'the person who rules both the king and the entire kingdom; he used to say "His Majesty will do so and so"'. In 1526, realising the danger of his ostentatious arrogance, Wolsey gave Hampton Court to King Henry VIII. It did not save him from disgrace.

Two of Henry's wives, Catherine Howard, who was beheaded, and Jane Seymour, the wife he truly loved, are said to haunt the building.

The buildings, with their sumptuous carvings, tapestries and grounds, are a magnificent reminder of the unparalleled extravagance of the age.

from **The Rape of The Lock**

Close by those meads for ever crowned with flow'rs,
Where Thames with pride surveys his rising tow'rs,
There stands a structure of majestic frame,
Which from the neighb'ring Hampton takes its name.
Here Britain's statesmen oft the fall foredoom
Of foreign tyrants, and of nymphs at home;
Here thou, great Anna! whom three realms obey,
Dost sometimes counsel take—and sometimes Tea

Alexander Pope, 1714

NOTES

James I

STUART LONDON
1603–1714

*A*t the beginning of the 17th century, under the first
monarch, James I (r.1603–1625), London had ceased
to be a medieval city. Heated largely by coal from Newcastle,
the capital was growing fast, pushing against its ancient
boundaries, and although the authorities passed injunctions
against new building, they were almost totally ignored. The
merchants of London were broadly Puritan and disliked the
autocratic Charles I and his Catholic wife. After Civil War
broke out in 1642, the City of London opposed the king
and strongly favoured Parliament, whose Roundhead army
could never have defeated the King's Cavaliers without the
city's support. Nevertheless, the Restoration of Charles II
(r.1660–85) was greeted by a great outburst of celebration in
London.

After the Great Fire of 1666 much of the city was rebuilt.
By the end of the 17th century London was laying
foundations for the financial supremacy that would lie at the
heart of the British Empire in the coming centuries.

NOTES ON
HISTORIC SITES

The Gunpowder Plot

After the accession of Protestant James I, English Catholics attempted the assassination of the new king and his Parliament. In 1605 Guy Fawkes tunnelled under the foundations of Parliament from a nearby house. With his conspirators he leased a cellar under the **House of Lords**, where they hid 36 barrels of gunpowder under a pile of brushwood. The attempt was foiled when the brushwood was searched. Guy Fawkes was seized and his fellow conspirators tried in vain to raise a rebellion. Fawkes was tortured and executed. His confession can be seen in the **Museum of the Public Record Office**. November 5 is still celebrated as Guy Fawkes Night, and there are bonfires and firework displays all over the country.

NOTES

The Civil War

Charles I believed in the God-given right of kings to rule over their nations, but his attempts to establish the sort of absolute personal rule that was common in Europe were fiercely resisted by Parliament. The King was determined to break this resistance by arresting the five most influential Members of Parliament who opposed him. In January 1642 the king and a band of armed men burst into the **House of Commons**. On being asked where the Members of Parliament were, the Speaker of the House, William Lenthall, replied, 'May it please your Majesty, I have neither eyes to see, nor tongue to speak in this place, but as the House is pleased to direct me, whose servant I am'– in fact the Members of Parliament had fled. After the King left London the five members returned from hiding in the city, amid scenes of wild celebration. The following summer Charles began raising troops, and when Parliament followed suit, England slipped into civil war. The King, without the support of the navy or the economic power of London, lost the war and signed a peace treaty. However, his constant plots to raise a fresh war against Parliament finally led to his trial and execution in 1649. It was the first time in history that a king was put on trial by the elected representatives of his people.

The Commonwealth and the Restoration

From 1649 to 1660 England was a Commonwealth presided over by Lord Protector Oliver Cromwell (1599–1658). In 1660 the monarchy was restored under Charles II. His triumphal entry into London was recorded by diarist of the period John Evelyn.

> This day his Majesty Charles II came to London after a sad and long exile, and calamitous suffering both of the King and Church, being seventeen years. This was also his birthday, and with a triumph of about 20,000 horse and foot, brandishing their swords and shouting with unexpressible joy; the ways strewed with flowers, the bells ringing, the streets hung with tapisserie, fountains running with wine; the Mayor, aldermen, and all the companies in their liveries, chains of gold, banners; lords and nobles cloth of silver, gold, and velvet everybody clad in; the windows and balconies all set with ladies; trumpets, music, and myriads of people flocking …
>
> John Evelyn, *Diary*, 29 May 1660

The Banqueting House

The Banqueting House in Whitehall was designed by Inigo
Jones (the king's surveyor) and finished in 1622.
Traditionally it is used for ceremonials, banquets, court
entertainments and formal receptions. The huge ceiling
paintings by Rubens were commissioned by Charles I in 1630
to commemorate his father, James I.

Covent Garden

Inigo Jones received a licence in 1631 to build and design London's first square. It was built on the grounds of an old monastery. The square, laid out in the Italian style, became known as Covent Garden. There has been a market on the site since the monks sold vegetables on the piazza in 1670. In later decades it became a lively vegetable and flower market. Samuel Pepys saw the first Punch and Judy show here and George Bernard Shaw used it for the setting of *Pygmalion*. Today it is the home of craftsmen and artists, who have daily market stalls. There are two fine museums to visit, the **London Transport Museum** and the **Theatre Museum**.

> Covent Garden ... a place with famous coffee-houses, where gentlemen wearing gold-laced coats and swords had quarrelled and fought duels ... a place where there was a nightly theatre, showing wonderful and beautiful sights to richly-dressed ladies and gentlemen ... desolate ideas of Covent Garden ... where the miserable children in rags ... like young rats, slunk and hid, fed on offal, huddled together for warmth, and were hunted about.
>
> Charles Dickens, *Little Dorrit*, 1855–67

St Paul's Cathedral

The masterpiece of late Stuart London is Christopher Wren's St Paul's Cathedral, built to replace the Old St Paul's Cathedral that was burnt down in the Great Fire. Started in 1675, building went on until 1710. This remarkable cathedral is loosely based on St Peter's in Rome, to which the great lead-covered dome is second only in size. The south tower contains the largest bell in England, Great Paul, which weighs 17 tons. The west facade, with its Baroque towers, is impressive when viewed at night.

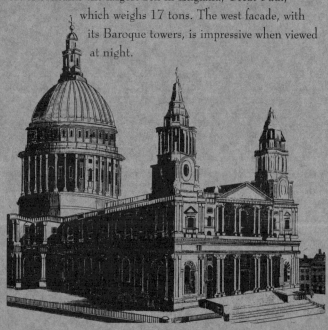

When the Surveyor in person [Christopher Wren] had set out upon the place the dimensions of the great dome, and fixed upon the centre, a common labourer was ordered to bring a flat stone from the heaps of rubbish (such as should first come to hand) to be laid for a mark and direction to the masons. The stone which was immediately brought and laid down for that purpose happened to be a piece of gravestone, with nothing remaining of the inscription but this single word in large capitals, RESURGAM [I will rise again].

Anon, 1670s

The word was emblazoned on the south transept of the new cathedral, above a figure of a phoenix rising from the ashes.

Sir Christopher Wren

Sir Christopher Wren (1632–1723) probably had more effect on the skyline of London than any other single man. After the Great Fire of 1666, Wren was appointed Surveyor-General. He drew up a plan for rebuilding the whole of the City of London using classical, French and Dutch influences, but the scheme was never undertaken. Instead he rebuilt in a more piecemeal manner 52 churches including **St Bride's**, **St Mary-le-Bow** (famous for Bow Bells), **St James's**, Piccadilly; and **St Stephen's**, Walbrook. In addition he left his mark on the **Royal Hospital, Chelsea**, **Hampton Court Palace** and, at Greenwich, the **Old Royal Observatory** and the **Royal Naval College**.

St Mary-Le-Bow

Greenwich

Greenwich is perhaps the best place to see Stuart London still intact. The Queen's House (1635), now the **National Maritime Museum**, is the work of Inigo Jones, and the **Old Royal Observatory** was built by Wren in 1675 – the zero meridian of longitude passes through it. The **Royal Naval College** was begun in 1696 and is the work first of Wren, then of his former assistant Nicholas Hawksmoor (1661–1736) and of the playwright turned architect Sir John Vanbrugh (1664–1726).

George I

GEORGIAN LONDON
1714–1837

*T*he 18th century was an age of great urban development. The population soared from 575,000 in 1700 to a million in 1815. The building of **Westminster Bridge** in 1750 and **Blackfriars Bridge** in 1763 encouraged rapid growth south of the river. As the centre of a rapidly expanding colonial empire, London became the world's busiest port.

Street lighting with oil lamps was introduced in 1750 and the sewerage system and public water supply were extended. London's shops were amongst the most dazzling in Europe, with one German visitor in 1786 describing how she window-shopped along the 'splendidly lit' **Oxford Street** until 11 o'clock at night. The other side of the coin was public squalor. As the Industrial Revolution transformed Britain the gap between rich and poor became increasingly apparent. Tensions grew and rioting broke out. During the Gordon Riots of 1780 a crowd of 50,000 spent five days in an orgy of looting and pillaging.

NOTES ON
HISTORIC SITES

Georgian buildings

Georgian architecture was based on classical traditions, and took its influence from ancient Rome, with plain but elegantly proportioned exteriors, colonnades and porticoes. The chief architectural players of the period were Nicholas Hawksmoor, Christopher Wren and John Nash. Among the surviving Georgian public buildings are **Horse Guards** at Whitehall (1755); originally York Place, guarded every day from 10am-4pm by soldiers (only members of the royal family are allowed to drive through the central arch); **Somerset House** (1796) in the Strand, the first large block of government offices ever built; and **Mansion House** (1752), the official residence of the Lord Mayor of London.

Somerset House

Fashionable London

Riches from all over the world flowed into London shops and markets. From New World spices, sugar, tobacco and chocolate to dazzling textiles from India and the Far East, London was the centre of taste and style. Elaborate homes and stately mansions encouraged the growth of fine craftsmanship and cabinet-makers like Chippendale, as well as silversmiths, mirror makers, glass workers and watchmakers, became famous throughout the world.

> We strolled up and down lovely Oxford Street this
> evening, for some goods look more attractive by
> artificial light. Just imagine, dear children, a street
> taking half an hour to cover from end to end ...
> and the pavement, inlaid with flagstones, can
> stand six people deep and allows one to gaze at the
> splendidly lit shop fronts in comfort. First one
> passes a watchmaker's, then a silk or fan store,
> now a silversmith's, a china or glass shop.
>
> Sophie von la Roche, on visiting Oxford Street, 1786,
> from *The Journal of Mary Frampton,*
> ed. Harriet Mundy, 1885

London's squares and terraces

The rich had always avoided living in the heart of London. However, the rapid growth of the city in the 17th and 18th centuries enveloped their mansions outside the city centre. The desire of the old aristocracy to move further afield, combined with the increasing wealth of some Londoners, and the destruction wreaked by the Great Fire, created a demand for new houses for the better-off. The first of these new developments was **Bloomsbury Square**, laid out in around 1670. **Soho Square** was built about 20 years later, (numbers 10 and 15 are original); other buildings date from the 18th and 19th centuries. **Hanover Square** (dating from around 1715), **Cavendish Square** (begun in the 1720s) and **Berkeley Square** (first laid out in the 1730s) all have fine early or mid-18th century houses. Later examples are **Bedford Square** (1780), a complete Georgian square, **Brunswick Square** (begun in the 1790s) and **Fitzroy Square**, finished in 1829.

Our part of London is so very superior to most others! – You must not confound us with London in general, my dear sir. The neighbourhood of Brunswick Square is very different from all the rest. We are so very airy! I should be unwilling, I own, to live in any other part of the town; there is hardly any other that I could be satisfied to have my children in; but we are so remarkably airy. Mr Wingfield thinks the neighbourhood of Brunswick Square decidedly the most favourable as to air.

Jane Austen, *Emma*, 1816

John Nash

If squares were the characteristic feature of London's development in the first half of the 18th century, terraces took over in the late 18th and early 19th centuries. The great exponent of this new style was John Nash, whose work includes **Great Cumberland Place** (1791), the **Haymarket Theatre** (1820) and the magnificent terraces and crescents around **Regent's Park** (1812–28). Nash is considered by many to be *the* London architect, who gave central London its shape, from the gardens and villas of **Regent's Park** to Portland Place, **Regent Street** and **Piccadilly Circus**.

IMPRESSIONS OF
SQUARES & STREETS

I have often amused myself with thinking how different a place London is to different people. They, whose narrow minds are contracted to the consideration of some one particular pursuit, view it only through that medium. A politician thinks of it merely as the seat of government in its different departments; a grazier, as a vast market for cattle; a mercantile man, as a place where a prodigious deal of business is done upon 'Change; a dramatick enthusiast, as the grand scene of theatrical entertainments; a man of pleasure, as an assemblage of taverns, and the great emporium for ladies of easy virtue. But the intellectual man is struck with it, as comprehending the whole of human life in all its variety, the contemplation of which is inexhaustible.

James Boswell, *Journal*, 1763

NOTES

James Boswell

Victoria

VICTORIAN &
EDWARDIAN LONDON
1837–1910

*D*uring the 19th century, under the long reign of
Queen Victoria (r.1837–1901), London's population
swelled to a staggering 6,500,000. Many of the city's parks
date from this period and were created to provide a 'lung' to
help the foul air circulate. Much of today's London is still
Victorian, and it was in the 19th century that the world's
image of London was formed. This was the London of
Charles Dickens and Sherlock Holmes, of the murderer Jack
the Ripper and swirling fogs; of miles of docks, the first
underground railway and the first tunnel under a river; of a
glittering theatre district and splendid and grandiose new
buildings. The period began with the rebuilding of the
Houses of Parliament in Gothic style, and encompassed the
opening of the **Royal Albert Hall** and the great department
stores such as **Harrods** and **Selfridges**. It also witnessed the
grinding poverty of the East End reach new depths.

NOTES ON
HISTORIC SITES

from **Don Juan**

A mighty mass of brick, and smoke, and shipping
   Dirty and dusky, but as wide as eye
Could reach, with here and there a sail just skipping
   In sight, then lost amidst the forestry
Of masts; a wilderness of steeples peeping
   On tiptoe through their sea-coal canopy;
A huge, dun cupola, like a foolscap crown
   On a fool's head – and there is London Town!

        Lord Byron, 1822

The Great Western Hotel, Paddington

Victorian buildings

Where Georgian architects looked back to Rome, Victorian architects were influenced by the style of the Middle Ages, including piers, spires, buttresses and pointed arches in their buildings. Fashionable Kensington has some fine examples of the large public buildings that are typical of Victorian architecture, including the **Victoria and Albert Museum** (1857) and the nearby **Natural History Museum** (1881) on Cromwell Road; the **Royal Albert Hall** (1871) in Kensington Gore; **St Pancras Station** (1868); and the **Albert Memorial** (1876) in Kensington Gardens. Victorian Gothic probably reached its peak in the **Law Courts** (1882), on the Strand. In 1812 the Gas-Light and Coke Co received a charter to provide the Corporation of London with gas street lighting.

Trafalgar Square and Nelson's Column

Trafalgar Square was created in 1824 to commemorate and honour the admiral who defeated Napoleon at the Battle of Trafalgar (1805), freeing the English from fear of attack by the Spanish and French. Trafalgar Square is one of London's most acclaimed architectural highlights. The fountains which appear here are a rarity in any London square. Today it is known chiefly as a tourist attraction and a meeting point for political demonstrations. Crowds gather in the square to celebrate New Year's Eve and Election Night and every year since World War II a Christmas tree sent from Norway is lit up here.

Nelson's Column in Trafalgar Square was erected in 1843. The statue of Nelson is 17 ft high. Around the base are reliefs of his four greatest victories, cast from cannons captured in battle by Nelson, and four huge statues of guardian lions.

The Savoy Hotel

One of the most sophisticated hotels in town opened its doors in 1884 to the rich and famous. Built to adjoin the **Savoy Theatre**, the hotel was the dream of opera impresario Richard D'Oyly Carte. The **Savoy Grill** remains one of London's best restaurants. Afternoon tea accompanied by the piano is part of this time-honoured institution's repertoire.

Cleopatra's Needle

The oldest public monument in London is Cleopatra's Needle on the Victoria Embankment. This Egyptian obelisk, dating from around 1475BC, was presented to the British in 1819 by the Turkish Viceroy of Egypt, but the problem of moving the 186-ton piece meant it did not reach London until 1878, having been almost lost in a storm in the Bay of Biscay. When it was erected many items were buried beneath it, including newspapers, money, china, a razor, cigars, Bibles, a picture of Queen Victoria, a railway guide, and photographs of 12 pretty Englishwomen of the day.

St Katherine's Dock

The London Docks were symbols of 19th-century London. St Katharine's Dock, like most of London's dockland, has been almost completely redeveloped in recent years, but the **Ivory House** (1860) remains, though now converted into flats. **The Dickens Inn** is in an old wooden warehouse. **Tobacco Dock** (1814) nearby has been partly protected and restored. Two huge warehouses (1825) are all that remain of the original West India Dock.

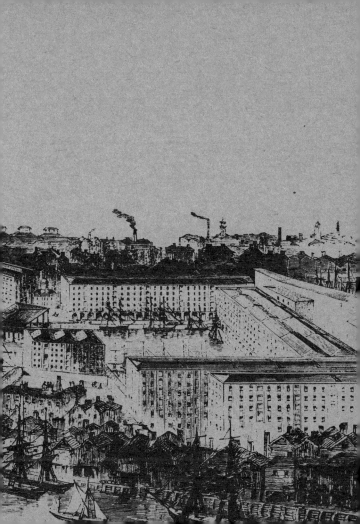

The railways

The arrival of the railways transformed London. The oldest
surviving locomotive, Stephenson's *Rocket* (1829) is in the
Science Museum. The first railway line reached London in
1836, and several railway termini are fine examples of
Victoriana: **King's Cross** (1852); **Paddington** (1854), the
work of Isambard Kingdom Brunel; **Charing Cross** (1864);
St Pancras (1868); and **Liverpool Street** (1874).

... the station of King's Cross had always
suggested infinity. Its very situation – withdrawn a
little behind the facile splendours of St Pancras –
implied a comment on the materialism of life.
Those two great arches, colourless, indifferent,
shouldering between them an unlovely clock, were
fit portals for some eternal adventure, whose issue
might be prosperous, but would certainly not be
expressed in the ordinary language of prosperity.

E M Forster, *Howards End*, 1910

The tube

London's first underground railway was the Metropolitan from Paddington to Farringdon Street, opened in 1863. On the first day over 30,000 people travelled on the trains and according to one source of the time, 'from nine o'clock in the morning till past midday it was impossible to obtain a place in the up or city-ward line at any of the mid stations. In the evening the tide turned … the report of the passengers was unanimous in favour of the smoothness and comfort of the line.' The first electric trains ran on the Northern line in 1890. Parts of several central London stations, notably the Circle Line platform at Baker Street, have been restored to their Victorian splendour.

NOTES

Winston Churchill

20TH-CENTURY LONDON

*D*ramatic social and economic changes have transformed London's landscape and brought a faster, more cosmopolitan way of life to the capital. The Suffragette campaign for votes for women in the early part of the century helped promote new liberal attitudes to women. The aftermath of World War I created a less socially divided, less restrained society. The wide spread destruction of World War II prompted a massive regeneration effort by the British government and for the first time women were a recognised and necessary part of the workforce.

The 1950s heralded the era of 'you've never had it so good', bringing material prosperity. Televisions, fridges, washing machines and cars brought new freedoms, an accelerated mode of living and improved worldwide communications. By the 1960s London was leading the fashion world with its popular street culture. Such social revolutions and a continuous transformation of fashions and tastes have super-imposed new ways of living on 2000 years of London life.

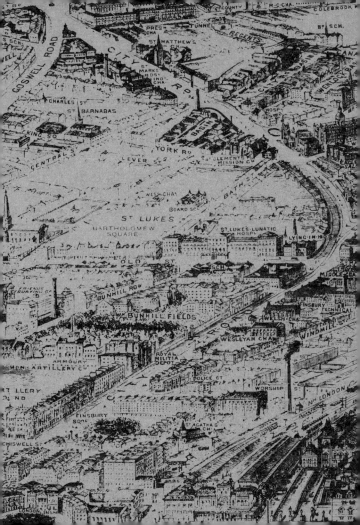

NOTES

The Blitz

From 1936 the British government worried about the implications for London in any war with Germany. It was predicted that the city would be virtually levelled to the ground by air raids, and with poison gas also expected, the authorities assumed civilian losses of around 19,000 a week. It was partly due to this fear that Britain and France gave way to Hitler at Munich in 1938. On the declaration of war, 90,000 women and children were evacuated from the city, though many returned. In fact, between September 1940 and May 1941 there were around 45,000 London casualties. The worst raid was on 10 May 1941, when 1436 people died.

LEAVE THIS TO US SONNY — <u>YOU</u> OUGHT TO BE OUT OF LONDON

MINISTRY OF HEALTH EVACUATION SCHEME

During 1944 London became the first city in history to come under long-range missile attack: 2500 V1 flying bombs, known to Londoners as doodlebugs or buzz-bombs because of the noise they made, killed over 6000 people. The V2 rockets, essentially the same as the first space rockets of the 1950s, were far more sophisticated. They reached speeds of 4000 mph and covered the 200 miles from the Netherlands to London in less than four minutes, coming down without a sound. The first landed in Chiswick on 8 September 1944 at 6.43pm; the second hit Epping a few seconds later. In all, about 500 V2s struck London, killing nearly 3000 people.

> The doodlebugs were much more frightening than bombs. I remember standing in the garden … then we heard the doodlebug. Zoom-zoom-zoom, zoom-zoom-zoom, and it cut out. There was nothing you could do. You didn't know where they'd come down. You just froze and waited, counting to three and hoping you were lucky.
>
> Monica Brown, speaking of her memories
> of a wartime childhood

Building boom

After the war, in 1951, the Festival of Britain ushered in the greatest building boom in the entire history of London. Many contemporary landmarks followed in the subsequent decades – the **South Bank Arts Centre**, the **Barbican**, new office buildings such as **Centre Point**, the **National Westminster Tower**, the new **Lloyds Building**, the redevelopment of docklands and the ambitious **Canary Wharf** office complex on the Thames. The population, too, has changed, with large-scale immigration from the Mediterranean, the Indian sub-continent and the Caribbean since World War II. Recent decades have witnessed a steady movement away from manufacturing and into services, with the City fighting to maintain its pre-eminence in finance. But the biggest employer of all has become the tourism industry.

The South Bank

The **Royal Festival Hall** is the chief surviving building from the Festival of Britain. It was the first building of the **South Bank Arts Centre**, which also includes the **National Film Theatre**, the **Queen Elizabeth Hall**, the **Purcell Room**, the **Hayward Gallery** (1968), the **Royal National Theatre** (1976) and the **Museum of the Moving Image** (1988).

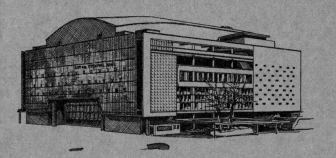

Queen Elizabeth Hall and the Purcell Room

Specialising in small orchestra performances, the Queen Elizabeth Hall is also used for performances catering for a diverse range of musical interests including jazz, ethnic music and modern interpretations of classic operas. The Purcell Room, more intimate than the Queen Elizabeth Hall, is used for chamber music concerts.

National Film Theatre

The National Film Theatre has catered for serious movie buffs since the early 1950s. A wide range of films, including regular screenings of cinematic rarities, are offered on two cinema screens.

The Barbican

Reflecting the age-old competition between the City of London and the areas south of the river, the City retaliated against the opening of the **South Bank Arts Centre** by building the **Barbican Arts Centre** (1982), with an art gallery, concert hall, three cinemas and two theatres. It is the London home of the **Royal Shakespeare Company** and the **London Symphony Orchestra**.

Contemporary buildings

Modern architecture in London ranges from the 800 ft
Canada Tower at **Canary Wharf** (1991) on the Thames at
the eastern edge of the City, to a brightly coloured
Stormwater Pumping Station (1988) on the Isle of Dogs.
Major buildings include Richard Rogers' **Lloyd's Building**
(1986), the development over **Charing Cross Station**
(1990) and **The Ark** (1992) in Hammersmith.

NOTES

PARTICULARITIES
of LONDON

FOG

*L*ondon was the first great city in history to be fuelled by coal. The combination of ever greater quantities of coal being burned by an expanding population, and London's naturally misty situation in a marshy river valley, meant London was plagued by regular fogs from Stuart times on. The worst lasted from November 1879 to March 1880 without a break.

In 1936-7, 322 tons of solid matter per square mile was deposited on Archbishop's Park, Lambeth, which meant nearly 30,000 tons of matter a year was deposited on London from the smoky atmosphere. At the same time central London received 18 per cent less sunshine than the inner suburbs. In 1934 there was fog from 10 November to 1 December, and deaths from respiratory diseases tripled. The fog of 1952 was estimated to have caused 4000 deaths. The Clean Air Act was passed in 1956, and the last great London fog was in 1962.

Fog everywhere. Fog up the river, where it flows among green aits and meadows; fog down the river, where it rolls defiled among the tiers of shipping and waterside pollutions of a great (and dirty) city ... fog lying out on the yards, and hovering in the rigging of great ships; fog drooping on the gunwales of barges and small boats. Fog in the eyes and throats of ancient Greenwich pensioners, wheezing by the firesides of their wards; fog in the stem and bowl of the afternoon pipe of the wrathful skipper, down in his close cabin; ... Chance people on the bridges peeping over the parapets into a nether sky of fog, with fog all round them, as if they were up in a balloon, and hanging in the misty clouds.

Charles Dickens, *Bleak House,* 1852-3

Notes

BUSES & TAXIS

The first rank for a Hackney Carriage (as London taxis are still called) was established in 1634 by St Mary-le-Strand. Hansom cabs were invented two centuries later, and motor taxis with taximeters were introduced in 1907. Before being allowed to operate, all taxi·drivers must pass a tough two-year examination (The Knowledge) to prove their familiarity with the city streets.

The first public transport in London was provided by horse-drawn buses in 1824, and motor omnibuses first ran in 1905. The red double-decker buses that are typical of London were designed in the 1930s and have continued happily with little change.

> London traffic, generally speaking and considering
> the fantastic pattern of the streets, is superbly
> managed. Of course the system wouldn't work in
> New York because it depends on a certain element
> of decency and obedience to the law.
>
> Raymond Chandler, *letter to Dale Warren*, 1952

GETTING AROUND

CEREMONY

*T*he British monarchy is one of the most enduring institutions in the world. Its ancestors were two 8th-century families, the Kings of Dalriada in western Scotland and the Kings of Wessex in southern England. Except for 11 years after the Civil War (1649–60), since the fall of the Roman Empire Britain has never been without at least one monarch. The pageantry of the Crown, and particularly the Coronation of a new monarch, dates back into the distant past, when it was used to overawe subjects, and provide the king with a semi-religious mystique. Subsequently the ceremonies became a way of symbolically uniting the nation.

London has its own unique ceremony, the **Lord Mayor's Show**, which has its roots in 1378, when the Lord Mayor of London led a procession to **Westminster Hall** to swear loyalty to the king. Since then this procession has been recreated annually with much pomp and ceremony.

NOTES

Trooping the Colour

Trooping the Colour takes place in the Horse Guards Parade on the second Saturday in June to honour the official birthday of the Sovereign.

The State Opening of Parliament

At the State Opening of Parliament the monarch arrives in the Irish State coach, escorted by the Household Cavalry. The ceremony is largely unchanged since the time of Elizabeth I. The monarch has never been allowed to enter the House of Commons since Charles I's disastrous visit in January 1642.

The Changing of the Guard

The Changing of the Guard at **Buckingham Palace** takes place around 11.30am in the grounds of the Palace, daily in the summer, every other day in the winter. The Horse Guards were established by Charles II to defend the now-vanished royal palace at Whitehall.

Buckingham Palace

Buckingham Palace was built in the early 19th century by John Nash. Queen Victoria was the first monarch to live there, and when she moved in it had faulty drains, bells that did not ring, doors that did not close, and windows that did not open. The Duke of Windsor, later briefly Edward VIII (r.1936) never liked it: 'The vast building with its stately rooms and endless corridors and passages, seemed pervaded by a curious, musty smell that still assails me whenever I enter its portals.' Part of the Palace is open to the public in the summer to raise money to pay for the damage caused by the recent Windsor Castle fire. The Royal Standard flies over Buckingham Palace when the Queen is in residence.

COCKNEYS

*L*ondoners are often called Cockneys. One 16th-century story is 'that a citizen's son riding with his father out of London into the country, and being a novice and ignorant of how corn or cattle increased, asked when he heard a horse neigh what the horse did. His father answered that "the horse does neigh". Riding further he heard a cock crow and said, "Does the cock neigh too?"' – hence 'cockney'. It is generally thought that the word actually comes from 'cokeney', meaning a cock's egg, thus implying a misshapen person or a fool. By tradition a cockney is anyone born within the sound of the bells of **St Mary-le-Bow**.

Cockney rhyming slang was originally a largely criminal dialect, designed to prevent the police and other outsiders from understanding. Its principle was that the slang word rhymed with what it actually meant. Examples are 'plates of meat' for 'feet'; 'apples and pears' for 'stairs'; and 'trouble and strife' for 'wife'.

NOTES

PUBS AND CLUBS

*P*ubs are London's true pulse. It is here where for centuries both Londoners and visitors have met to drink, talk, laugh, argue, smoke and share gossip. Pubs are 'public houses' licensed for the public consumption of alcohol. Pubs are strictly licensed and must keep particular hours. Many pubs are owned by breweries who maintain high standards for both drink and decor.

In London there is a sharp difference between pubs and clubs, even though both are largely used for social drinking. Clubs are for private members only, and range from centuries-old semi-political institutions like **White's** to the recently established **Groucho's**, where literary and media figures gather. There are also music venues with flexible membership, like **Ronnie Scott's**, the **Jazz Café**, **The Forum** and **The Ministry of Sound**.

Favourite Pubs

Early Pubs

Many early London pubs attracted a particular clientele. Public houses provided the ambience and settings in which conspiracies were hatched, disputes judged, military plans made, politicians lobbied, and new ideas bandied. Above all many pubs were magnets for literary figures of the day. At the now demolished Mermaid pub, Sir Walter Raleigh founded a club whose membership included John Donne, Shakespeare, and many others. Keats commemorated this tradition in 1818 in a famous poem:

> *from* **Lines on the Mermaid Tavern**
>> Souls of Poets dead and gone,
>>> What Elysium have ye known,
>>> Happy field or mossy cavern,
>>>> Choicer than the Mermaid Tavern?

Prospect of Whitby

The oldest riverside inn in London is the Prospect of Whitby in Wapping Wall. It was built in 1520, when it was known as the Devil's Tavern and popular with thieves and smugglers. It changed its name in 1777 because a ship called the Prospect from Whitby regularly moored just outside it. Famous customers included Dickens, Pepys, Whistler and Turner.

George Inn

The only galleried coaching inn left in London is the George Inn, Borough High Street. Originally called the St George, and dating from at least 1542, it was burnt down in 1670 and rebuilt six years later on the old plan. In summer, following medieval traditions, play performances are often given in the inn yard.

Ye Olde Cheshire Cheese

Ye Olde Cheshire Cheese in Wine Office Court, off Fleet Street, used to be the most popular pub among journalists. It has been famous for centuries for its delicious servings of steak and kidney pies, oysters and mushrooms. It was described in the early 19th century as 'a little lop-sided, wedged-up house, that always reminds you structurally of a high-shouldered man with his hands in his pockets. It is full of holes and corners and cupboards and sharp turnings; and … you must tread cautiously if you would not wish to be tripped up by plates and dishes momentarily deposited there by furious waiters…' This pub was well known as a meeting place for such literary luminaries as Samuel Johnson, James Boswell, and in later years Dickens and Conan Doyle.

The Cock Tavern

The Cock Tavern, Fleet Street, was built in 1887 to replace a 16th-century inn of the same name. Pepys went there on 23 April 1668 with three actresses and 'drank, and ate a lobster, and sang and mightily merry'. Taking one of the women home, he then had to avoid 'two rogues with clubs', and finally went to bed annoyed at how much he had spent. Tennyson frequented The Cock and included it in *Will Waterproof's Lyrical Monologue*, written during the 1830s:

> O plump head-waiter at The Cock,
>   To which I most resort,
> How goes the time? 'Tis five o'clock.
>   Go fetch a pint of port.

The Black Friar

The Black Friar, Queen Street, is on the site of the Blackfriars Monastery. It was built in 1875 and remodelled 30 years later with mosaics and carved figures of monks. It has a grotto built into the vaults of the neighbouring railway.

The Spaniards Inn

The Spaniards Inn in Hampstead Lane is said to have been named after two 17th-century Spanish brothers who owned the inn, and killed each other in a duel over a woman. The highwayman Dick Turpin (1705–39) drank here and stabled his horse, Black Bess, opposite. Famous patrons have included Shelley, Keats, Byron, Joshua Reynolds and the actor David Garrick.

Clubs

Clubs became fashionable at the end of the Stuart monarchy, where like-minded gentlemen could meet in appropriately elegant masculine settings to eat, drink, gamble, gossip and make deals. Many clubs originated in taverns, coffee houses and chocolate houses and then moved to large private homes.

> The club question had become serious and difficult; a club was indispensable, but I had of course none of my own … At last, I forget exactly when, I was elected to the Reform; … This was an excellent piece of good fortune, and the Club has ever since been, to me, a convenience of the first order. I could not have remained in London without it, and I have become extremely fond of it; a deep local attachment.
>
> Henry James, *Notebooks*, 1881

White's

White's club at 37 St James's Street started out in 1693 as White's Chocolate House. It was the political Tory Club and long famous for gambling and loose morality. On 1 September 1750 a man collapsed outside the club and was carried in. Members immediately made bets as to whether he was dead or not, and objected to any treatment for him as it would affect the fairness of the bet.

Prince Charles held his stag night at White's in 1981. Other well-known clubs include **Brooks'** (1764), also in St James's, and the **Travellers'** (1819), **Athenaeum** (1824), and **Reform Club** (1836) in Pall Mall. The last was made famous by Jules Verne in *Around the World in Eighty Days*.

Boodle's

Boodle's club, founded in 1763, is at 28 St James's Street. No one knows who Boodle was, but the club has always been famous for its food.

To make the famous Boodle's Orange Fool, squeeze the juice of four oranges and two lemons, add some grated rind and mix with sugar to taste. Cut six small sponge cakes into four pieces each and put them in a dish. Pour a pint of cream into the fruit juice, stirring lightly; pour this mixture over the cakes, leave for 2–4 hours, then serve.

THEATRES

William Shakespeare

*L*ondon has consistently been one of the most important centres in the world for live theatre. The first purpose-built theatre was put up in 1576 in Finsbury Fields, and began the four century-long tradition of London's theatres. From Shakespeare and the Globe, through actors like Garrick and Irving to today, London is the only city in the world used by two internationally famous repertory theatres – the **Royal National Theatre** and the **Royal Shakespeare Company**. London's theatre-land, basically the West End around Shaftesbury Avenue and the Strand, contains 42 theatres, showing musicals, classical dramas and new plays. In addition there are large numbers of 'fringe' theatres where small companies, and even single actors, put on low-budget and experimental productions. A number of pubs scattered around London, like the **Orange Tree** in Richmond, and the **King's Head** in Islington, show small-scale theatre productions at lunchtime or evenings.

NOTES ON
THEATRES & PLAYS

Elizabethan drama

England's remarkable dramatic flowering in Elizabethan times was a result of a number of wide-ranging developments. The early church traditions of drama, which included nativity plays and mystery cycles, naturally transformed into a more secular experience as the power of the Catholic church was destroyed. In addition popular entertainments such as troubadours, bear baiting, cock fighting, early pub plays and 'interludes', prepared the stage for communal entertainment in a fixed setting. Moreover, the Protestant church strongly encouraged bible study and as such helped to create a literate populace ready to read Shakespeare's first folios. This was supported by major advances in the printing and publishing industry in London. Finally, there was a natural audience in London for plays and entertainment, drawn from the thousands of lawyers studying at the **Inns of Court**, from London's aldermen, councillors and parliamentarians, from the personages associated with the courts, as well as from local Londoners and foreign visitors.

The Globe Theatre

The Globe Theatre, famous for staging most of Shakespeare's greatest plays, was burnt to the ground in 1613 during a performance of Shakespeare's *Henry VIII*, when the firing of two cannons set the thatch alight. No one was hurt except for one man who had 'his breeches on fire that would perhaps have broiled him if he had not with the benefit of a provident wit put it out with bottle ale'. Just by its original site at Bear Gardens, the Globe Theatre has now been rebuilt. This remarkably true to the times theatre houses a permanent exhibition and produces period performances during the summer season.

To the King's playhouse, and there saw *Henry IV*
... The house full of Parliament men, it being
holiday with them: and it was observable how a
gentleman of good habit, sitting just before us,
eating of some fruit in the midst of the play, did
drop down as dead, being choked; but with much
ado Orange Moll did thrust her finger down his
throat, and brought him to life again.

Samuel Pepys, *Diary*, 2 November 1667

The Royal National Theatre

The Royal National Theatre on the South Bank opened in 1976 in the teeth of media criticism. Sir Peter Hall, the director recorded: 'Architecturally it is going to be wonderful. It is not palatial, but human. The roof is not yet on and the concrete is raw and rude. But one can feel the intimacy of the place.' The complex houses three theatres – **The Olivier**, **The Cottesloe** and the **Lyttleton**, and produces some of the best that London theatre can offer.

The Royal Shakespeare Company

Britain's other royal theatre company has its London home at the Barbican Centre. As its name suggests, the company is synonymous with first-class presentations of Shakespeare's work. Lavish productions can be seen at the **Barbican Theatre**, while smaller productions of modern works can be enjoyed at **The Pit**.

STREET VENDORS,
FAIRS AND MARKETS

*L*ondon has always had a huge variety of street vendors, stalls, fairs and markets. The fairs were mostly stopped in Victorian times, because of the rowdiness they caused, and over the last century the number of street vendors, or costermongers as they were known, has dropped sharply, but many markets still remain. Flower stalls are common, and one outside Waterloo Station provided a living for many years for one of the 'great train robbers' after he was released from prison. Gypsies still sell 'lucky white heather' in parts of central London; bags of chestnuts, roasted in braziers before your eyes, can be bought on the streets in autumn and winter.

Many visitors come to London with antiques and bric-a-brac in mind and one can hear an international polyphony of bargaining any day of the week at market stalls scattered from one end of London to the other.

NOTES

Street cries

The disappearance of most London street vendors has meant the disappearance of the street cries they used to publicise their goods, and the only common one left is the shout of 'Stan-dard' by sellers of London's local paper. It was very different when Joseph Addison wrote his essay on the subject in the early 18th century: 'There is nothing which more astonishes a foreigner and frights a country squire than the Cries of London. Milk is generally sold in a note above all else and it sounds so exceeding shrill that it often sets our teeth on edge.'

Nonetheless the tradition remains in the street markets and one has just to visit **Chapel Market**, for example, any morning of the week (except Monday) to hear the cries selling fish, flowers, penny candy, hardware, fruit, fake Rolex's, vegetables, men's socks and anything else one could ever need.

Camden Lock

Just north of Regent's Park is Camden Lock, where the Grand Union Canal runs under Camden High Street. In 1951 Baedecker dismissed it as 'a shabby district', but in recent years it has become one of the most lively parts of London. There are art and craft shops, antiques, designer clothes, galleries, music shops, jewellery stalls, secondhand books, together with the famous live music club, **Dingwalls**, where many rock, blues and jazz legends have performed. Visit on the weekend and come early.

Smithfield

Smithfield Market dates from the 12th century, when it was used for the sale of horses, and the site of the famous annual Bartholomew Fair, suppressed by the city authorities in 1855. The area was used for tournaments and public executions. By the 17th century it was London's chief meat market, as it still is. Until 1855 Smithfield was also the largest live market in the world: 'the noise was deafening. The bellowing and lowing of cattle, bleating of sheep, squeaking of pigs, the shouts of the drovers and often the shrieks of some unfortunate female who had got amongst the unruly, frightened cattle, could not be forgotten.' The new building for the market was opened in 1867.

Billingsgate

Billingsgate Market on Lower Thames Street was the fish market of London for centuries. It existed as a market from at least 1016, and in 1698 it was made 'a free and open market for all sorts of fish'. The leather hats worn by fish porters there were based on the helmets worn by the English bowmen at the Battle of Agincourt (1415). In 1870 an American described 'the famous Billingsgate Fish Market, which has given or originated a synonym for blackguardism and low abuse all the world over'. The present market building was opened in 1877, but the fish market moved to the Isle of Dogs in 1982, and the building is now used as an international banking centre.

To look down it [Petticoat Lane Market] is to look down a vista of many-coloured garments, alike on the sides and on the ground. The effect sometimes is very striking, from the variety of hues, and the constant flitting or gathering of the crowd into little groups of bargainers. Gowns of every shade and every pattern are hanging up, but none, perhaps, look either bright or white; it is a vista of dinginess, but many-coloured dinginess.

Henry Mayhew, *London Labour and the London Poor* (1851–2)

Bermondsey Market

Early Friday mornings, this premier London antiques market is groaning with everything from solid oak armoires to lace doilies and weather-beaten picture frames to solid brass binoculars and porcelain teapots. There are many antique stores open all week nearby.

Camden Passage

This charming street passage off Upper Street in Islington is a mecca for antique textiles, jewellery, clothing, furniture, silver and porcelain. Open every Wednesday and Saturday morning, it is possible to find a Georgian silver tea-service, rare prints, fabulous old Liberty silk scarves, among other treasures. While here have a meal at **Frederick's** or the charming **Trattoria Aquilino** and watch the world go by. The excellent **Craft Council Gallery** is only a few blocks away.

Portobello Market

Portobello Road Market was begun in the 1870s by gypsies. The market caused much trouble, and not until 1929 was a licence granted for it. Since 1948 it has been chiefly an antiques market, with the main market on Saturdays. This is one of London's top antiques and collectables marketplaces and is a good place to hunt for textiles, jewellery and wonderful souvenirs.

Notes

GREAT LONDON
EVENTS

PLAGUES

*H*ygiene in London was largely non-existent until the 19th century, and the huge number of people living crammed tightly together made disease a constant danger. The bubonic plagues of 1348 and 1665 were spread by fleas carried by the black rats that swarmed in London. The arrival of brown rats, who drove out the black rats, may have helped end the bubonic plague. Many think the Great Fire of 1666 smoked out the plague. Other diseases flourished in London, including leprosy, widespread in medieval times but then stamped out, cholera, which was especially virulent during the early-19th century, typhus, typhoid, various fevers, dysentery, and smallpox. London was well known as the most sickly place in the kingdom, a place where as one letter writer put it 'they die fast'.

Notes

THE GREAT FIRE

Samuel Pepys

*I*n 1657 it was authoritatively stated that 'there's no place better armed against the fury of the fire' than London. Nine years later, a little before two o'clock in the morning of 2 September, a workman in a bakery in Pudding Lane smelled smoke and woke the house. Sparks blown by a strong easterly wind crossed the street and set alight an inn yard where hay was stacked. From then on the flames spread rapidly and unstoppably. Before burning itself out, the fire lasted over three days, covering the area from the Tower to Fleet Street and from the Thames to Moorfields, destroying 80 per cent of the City of London. Incredibly few people died in the conflagration, one of them a maid from the bakery where the fire started. Over 13,000 houses and 87 churches were destroyed, and up to 200,000 people made homeless.

Everybody endeavouring to remove their goods, and flinging into the river or bringing them into lighters that lay off; poor people staying in their houses as long as till the very fire touched them, and then running into boats, or clambering from one pair of stairs, by the waterside, to another. And among other things, the poor pigeons, I perceive, were loth to leave their houses, but hovered about the windows and balconies, till they burned their wings and fell down. Having stayed, and in an hour's time seen the fire rage every way; and nobody, to my sight, endeavouring to quench it, but to remove their goods, and leave all to the fire; and having seen it get as far as the Steel Yard, and the wind mighty high, and driving it into the City: and everything, after so long a drought, proving combustible, even the very stones of churches.

Samuel Pepys, *Diary*, 2 September 1666

Monument

The Monument in Monument Street, designed by Christopher Wren, was built in 1677 to commemorate the Great Fire. It is 202 ft high, and 202 ft from the site of the baker's house in Pudding Lane where the Great Fire broke out. Inside is a staircase of 345 steps. At the top is an urn, though Wren had wanted a colossal brass statue of Charles II. On the west side an inscription blamed the fire on 'the treachery and malice' of the Roman Catholics, and 'their horrid plot for the extirpating the Protestant religion and English liberties, and to introduce Popery and slavery', but this was removed in 1831.

The Thames
& its Bridges

Swans

The first proof of swan-keeping on the Thames in London comes in 1246, when swans were used for food and sold in the open market. The price of a swan in the 14th century was 4 or 5 shillings (20–25p), nearly ten times that of a goose or duck. In 1496 the secretary to the Venetian ambassador wrote, 'it is truly a beautiful thing to behold one or two thousand tame swans upon the river Thames'.

> How beautiful did Old Father Thames look yesterday—it was prettily scattered about with swans above Richmond—and when they flew over the water, the clapping of their wings was very loud indeed.
>
> John Constable, letter to C R Leslie, RA,
> 8 September 1834

Painting the river

I tried again and again to capture the Thames in a painting, the artery of life flowing from century to century, the river beside which multitudes gathered to form a community with a style of life all its own, bringing the most diverse races together in a way that can be paralleled only perhaps in the ancient states of Asia, in China, or in the old Danubian monarchy.

Oskar Kokoschka, 1967

Where the process became really awful was on the Thames. Appearance changed all the time. At the Savoy Hotel or at St Thomas's Hospital, where I had my viewpoints, I kept almost a hundred canvases on the go – for one subject. I would search feverishly through my sketches till I found one not too different from what I could see. Then in spite of everything I would change it entirely. When I finished work, I would move the canvases and see that I had overlooked just the one which would have served – there it was in my hand. That wasn't very bright!

Claude Monet, from an interview published in 1927
La Reine de l'art ancien et moderne

Notes

The oldest bridge in London

The oldest surviving bridges in London are well upstream. Clattern Bridge at Kingston dates from the 12th century; Richmond is the oldest Thames bridge (built 1774–7), followed by Kingston (1828). Some remains of the original medieval bridge at Kingston have been incorporated in the John Lewis store on the riverside. Virtually all central London bridges have been rebuilt at least twice, and most of the oldest remaining are railway bridges – **Barnes** (1849), **Blackfriars** (1864) and **Charing Cross** (1864). Other 19th-century bridges are **Westminster**, built to replace the old unstable bridge in 1862, **Albert** (1873), **Hammersmith** (1883), **Putney** (1886), **Battersea** (1890), and **Tower Bridge** (1894).

Westminster Bridge

Earth has not anything to show more fair:
  Dull would he be of soul who could pass by
A sight so touching in its majesty:
  This City now doth, like a garment, wear
The beauty of the morning; silent, bare,
  Ships, towers, domes, theatres, and temples lie
Open unto the fields, and to the sky;
  All bright and glittering in the smokeless air.
Never did sun more beautifully steep
  In his first splendour, valley, rock, or hill;
Ne'er saw I, never felt, a calm so deep!
  The river glideth at his own sweet will:
Dear God! the very houses seem asleep;
  And all that mighty heart is lying still!

William Wordsworth, composed upon
Westminster Bridge, 1807

We mounted the Dover Coach at Charing Cross.
It was a beautiful morning. The City, St Pauls,
with the River and a multitude of little Boats,
made a beautiful sight as we crossed Westminster
Bridge. The houses were not overhung by their
cloud of smoke and they were spread out endlessly,
yet the sun shone so brightly and with such a pure
light that there was even something like the purity
of one of nature's own grand spectacles.

Dorothy Wordsworth, *Journals, 1802*

Tower Bridge

The best-known of London's bridges is Tower Bridge. It was built to allow large ships access to the city and to provide a river crossing close to the expanding docks. Opened by the Prince of Wales, later Edward VII, in 1894, it cost over a million pounds to build. The Gothic-style towers contain lifts which once carried pedestrians up to the high-level walkway. The bridge rises once a day at high water. In 1953 a double-decker bus 'jumped' across the bridge as it was opening.

LITERARY
LONDON

Literary Associations

The literary associations of London begin with the Londoner Geoffrey Chaucer (c.1340–1400), and the gathering of his 14th-century Canterbury pilgrims at the now-vanished Tabard Inn in Southwark. All of Shakespeare's plays were performed in London, where he also acted; the incredibly prolific Daniel Defoe (c.1660–1731) was born, educated and died in London; Samuel Johnson (1709–84) insisted that there was no place in the world to compare with London; Leigh Hunt (1784–1859), the 'cockney poet', settled in the West End and included John Keats (1795–1821) among his circle. **Keats House** in Hampstead is where the poet wrote many of his finest works. Charles Dickens' most impressive novels all include extensive London scenes; Oscar Wilde (1854–1900) was a dedicated Londoner until his imprisonment; George Bernard Shaw (1856–1950) spent much of his life in London and put the city into many of his plays; the early 20th-century writers Virginia Woolf, Lytton Strachey and their circle took their name, the Bloomsbury Group, from part of London; in *Down and Out in Paris and London* (1933) George Orwell draws on his experiences of living among London tramps. The list is almost endless.

Separate from the pleasure of your company, I don't much care if I never see a mountain in my life. I have passed all my days in London, until I have formed as many and intense local attachments, as any of your mountaineers can have done with dead nature. The Lighted shops of the Strand and Fleet Street; the innumerable trades, tradesmen and customers, coaches, waggons, playhouses; all the bustle and wickedness round about Covent Garden, the very women of the Town, the watchmen, drunken scenes, rattles, – life awake, if you awake, at all hours of the night, the impossibility of being dull in Fleet Street, the crowds, the very dirt and mud, the Sun shining upon houses and pavements, the print shops, the old book stalls, parsons cheap'ning books, coffee houses, steams of soup from kitchens, the pantomimes, London itself a pantomime and a masquerade ...

Letter from Charles Lamb to
William Wordsworth, 1801

LITERARY LONDON

Diarists and chroniclers of London

The first chronicler of London life was William Fitzstephen, a late 12th-century monk, whose description of the city, which he obviously knew well and loved, occurs as a preface to his *Life of Thomas à Becket*.

The most famous writers about London lived in the 17th, 18th and 19th centuries. *The Diaries of John Evelyn* cover the period from 1631 to 1706, for much of which he lived in London and observed nearly all the great events of the time. His diary was discovered by accident in a clothes basket in 1817. Samuel Pepys was an important politician, whose diary, written in a secret code that was only deciphered in 1825, covered the years 1660–69, giving a fascinating view of the world of London's ruling class in the mid-17th century. James Boswell, the biographer of Samuel Johnson, was a Scotsman who wrote a famously detailed diary of his doings in London from his first arrival there in November 1762 to August 1763, including frequent descriptions of his love affairs and visits to London prostitutes.

John Evelyn

In the 19th century London became the greatest city the world had yet seen, and a source of great fascination at home and abroad. Henry Mayhew's *London Labour and the London Poor* (1851) documented the life of the poor in the city in exhaustive detail. The French writer Blanchard Jerrold produced *London, a Pilgrimage* (1872), with superb illustrations by Gustave Doré showing every aspect: the tea-parties of the rich aristocracy as well as the thieves' 'kitchens' of the East End. At the same time the American journalist Daniel Joseph Kirwan, in *Palace and Hovel* (1870), documented London from Buckingham Palace and the dubious doings of the Prince of Wales to the wretched men who made a living by scavenging in the London sewers.

Amid the noble cities of the world, the City of London, throne of the English kingdom, is one which has spread its fame far and wide, its wealth and merchandise to great distances, raised its head on high. It is blessed by a wholesome climate, blessed too in Christ's religion, in the strength of its fortifications, in the nature of its site, the repute of its citizens, the honour of its matrons; happy in its sports, prolific in noble men.

William Fitzstephen, Preface to the
Life of Thomas à Becket, c.1180

Charles Dickens

Charles Dickens (1812–70) is probably the most famous writer about London, and his descriptions of the city in the middle of the 19th century established a view that has almost become a cliché. He was born in Portsmouth, but the family moved to London when Dickens was only nine. A year later his father was put in prison for debt and Dickens was forced to work labelling bottles of blacking. The family suffered hardship until Dickens became a full-time journalist when he was 22. His first book was published two years later. Among the famous descriptions of the capital in his books are the Fleet prison in *Pickwick Papers* (begun in 1836), Fagin's den in *Oliver Twist* (1837–9), the Gordon Riots in *Barnaby Rudge* (1841), the Thames boatmen searching for corpses in *Our Mutual Friend* (1864–5), Dickens's own experiences in the Blackfriars blacking factory in *David Copperfield* (1849–50), and an opium den in the London docks in *Edwin Drood* (1870), left unfinished.

It was a very dark night. The day had been unfavourable, and at that hour and place there were few people stirring. Such as there were, hurried quickly past: very possibly without seeing, but certainly without noticing, either the woman, or the man who kept her in view. Their appearance was not calculated to attract the importunate regards of such of London's destitute population, as chanced to take their way over the bridge that night in search of some cold arch or doorless hovel wherein to lay their heads; they stood there in silence: neither speaking nor spoken to, by any one who passed.

A mist hung over the river, deepening the red glare of the fires that burnt upon the small craft moored off the different wharfs, and rendering darker and more indistinct the mirky buildings on the banks. The old smoke-stained storehouses on either side, rose heavy and dull from the dense mass of roofs and gables, and frowned sternly upon water too black to reflect even their lumbering shapes.

Charles Dickens, *Oliver Twist*, 1837

Sir Arthur Conan Doyle and Sherlock Holmes

The literary vision of London created by Dickens, of fog, wretched poverty, the docks and hansom cabs, was cemented half a century later by Sir Arthur Conan Doyle (1859–1930). He was born in Edinburgh and moved to London to become an oculist. While waiting for patients he used the time to write – the result was the first modern detective, Sherlock Holmes, with his home at 221b Baker Street. **The Sherlock Holmes Museum**, situated between No 237 and No. 239 Baker Street, recreates the great detective's lodgings from descriptions in the stories.

It was a bright crisp February morning, and the snow of the night before still lay deep upon the ground, shimmering brightly in the wintry sun. Down the centre of Baker Street it had been ploughed into a brown crumbly band by the traffic, but at either side and on the heaped-up edges of the footpaths it still lay as white as when it fell … no one was coming save the single gentleman whose eccentric conduct had drawn my attention … "I believe that he is coming here," said Holmes, rubbing his hands.

Arthur Conan Doyle, *The Beryl Coronet*, 1892

Bloomsbury Group

In the early 20th century a group of friends, mostly writers and artists, formed a united group subscribing to the philosophy that human friendships and beautiful objects are a rational conclusion of social progress. Among the most influential of the group were Virgina Woolf, Lytton Strachey, Roger Fry, Vanessa and Clive Bell, E M Forster, John Maynard Keynes, David Garnett and Duncan Grant.

But how strange, on entering the Park, the silence; the mist; the hum; the slow-swimming happy ducks; the pouched birds waddling; and who should be coming along with his back against the Government buildings, most appropriately, carrying a despatch box stamped with the Royal Arms, who but Hugh Whitbread; her old friend Hugh – the admirable Hugh!

"Good-morning to you, Clarissa!" said Hugh, rather extravagantly, for they had known each other as children. "Where are you off to?"

"I love walking in London," said Mrs Dalloway. "Really, it's better than walking in the country."

Virginia Woolf, *Mrs Dalloway*, 1925

NOTES

Artists & Music in London

William Hogarth

ARTISTS IN LONDON

*T*he first great illustrator of London was the Bohemian Wenceslaus Hollar (1607–77), whose precise drawings and engravings reveal the vanished London of the 1640s, before the Great Fire. During the next century the paintings, engravings and cartoons of Hogarth (1697–1764) and Rowlandson (1756–1827) exposed the seamier side of London, while Canaletto (1697–1768) showed a picture more in keeping with the pure classical architecture of the time. 19th-century artists were fascinated by London as the massive industrial heartland of the world, lost in grey and yellow fogs. Those who painted impressions of the capital at this time were Turner (1775–1851), Monet (1840–1926), Pissarro (1830–1903), Sisley (1839–99) and the American Whistler (1834–1903). 20th-century painters of London have included the Camden Town Group and foreign visitors like André Derain (1880–1954) and Oskar Kokoschka (1886–1980).

J M Turner

NOTES

Court painters

The great painters of the 16th and 17th centuries came from abroad, and their works are mainly portraits of royalty and noblemen of the time. Hans Holbein (c.1497–1543) from Germany settled in England permanently from 1532. His drawings can be seen in **The Queen's Gallery** at Buckingham Palace, and his paintings at the **National Gallery** and **National Portrait Gallery**. The Flemish artists Peter-Paul Rubens (1577–1640) and Anthony van Dyck (1599–1641) were court painters to Charles I. Their work can be seen at the **Courtauld Institute**, **Dulwich Picture Gallery**, **Kensington Palace**, **Lancaster House**, the **National Gallery**, the **National Portrait Gallery**, the **Tate Gallery** and the **Wallace Collection**. Rubens' ceiling paintings for the **Banqueting House**, Whitehall, are especially remarkable. Later court painters included Peter Lely (1618–80) and Godfrey Kneller (c.1649–1723), whose works can be seen at **Ham House**, the **National Maritime Museum** and the **Tate Gallery**.

And when the evening mist clothes the riverside
with poetry, as with a veil, and the poor buildings
lose themselves in the dim sky, and the tall
chimneys become campanili, and the warehouses
are palaces in the night, and the whole city hangs
in the heavens, and fairy-land is before us ... and
Nature, who, for once, has sung in tune, sings her
exquisite song to the artist alone ...

James McNeill Whistler,
The Gentle Art of Making Enemies, 1890

Impressionists in London

In 1870 I found myself in London with Monet, and we met Daubigny and Bonvin. Monet and I were very enthusiastic over the London landscapes. Monet worked in the parks, whilst I, living at Lower Norwood, at that time a charming suburb, studied the effects of fog, snow, and springtime: We worked from Nature, and later on Monet painted in London some superb studies of mist. We also visited the museums. The water-colours and paintings of Turner and of Constable, the canvases of Old Crome, have certainly had influence upon us. We admired Gainsborough, Lawrence, Reynolds, etc., but we were struck chiefly by the landscape painters, who shared more in our aim with regard to *plein air*, light, and fugitive effects. Watts, Rossetti, strongly interested us amongst the modern men. About this time we had the idea of sending our studies to the exhibitions of the Royal Academy. Naturally we were rejected.

Camille Pissarro, letter to Wynford Dewhurst, 1904

The Arts and Crafts Movement

The Arts and Crafts Movement, pioneered by William Morris, has left several marks on London, the best example probably being **Holy Trinity Church** in Sloane Street, begun in 1890. The pre-Raphaelite painter, Lord Leighton, often known as the 'high priest of the cult of the occult', left his **Leighton House** (1866) as a monument to the genre. Here it is possible to see the brilliant tiles of William de Morgan and the Arab Hall, created complete with a central fountain and beautiful mosaics. It was an admirable spot for the Lord and his friends to indulge in one of the favourite pleasures of the day, smoking opium. Nearby **Tower House** (1881), Melbury Road, is an extraordinary example of domestic Victorian Gothic architecture.

Liberty of London

This glorious mock-Tudor style shop in the heart of London has been a beacon for fashion since Arthur Lasenby opened his doors in 1875. Liberty fabrics, furniture and jewellery, often designed by leading artists of the day like William Morris, contributed to the ongoing success and strength of the Arts and Crafts movement. The shop, with its delightful restaurants, bookshop, glittering jewellery cases, designer clothing, oriental rug bazaar and much more, is a mecca for Londoners and visitors alike.

MUSIC IN LONDON

Henry Purcell

The traditions of music in London go back to the Middle Ages when City churches organised regular lunchtime concerts. Music was a regular part of Christian worship and a strong part of early London street life. The first great period of music in London lasted from about 1680 to 1820, beginning with the Londoner Henry Purcell (c. 1659–95). The arrival of the Hanoverian kings in the 18th century led to a close link with Germany. The greatest composer to do most of his work in London was Handel (1685–1759). Johann Christian Bach (1735–82) spent much of his life in London, and Haydn (1732–1809) and Mozart (1756–91) visited the capital. The operettas of two Londoners, William Gilbert (1836–1911) and Arthur Sullivan (1842–1900), which included *The Yeoman of the Guard*, opened in London in the late 19th century. In the 1960s London became the rock capital of the world with an explosion of music by groups such as the Rolling Stones.

NOTES ON CONCERTS

The Royal Opera House

The Royal Opera House, Covent Garden, is the most famous home of music in London, and virtually every major opera singer has performed here. There has been a theatre on the site since 1732 – the present one opened in 1858, though the frieze behind the portico, dating from 1809, was saved from the previous building. During the 19th century according to social historian Blanchard Jerrold, 'beyond all doubt the amusement that delights the largest number of the cultivated in London is the opera', but it did mean 'you must be in full dress swallow-tail and white choker'.

The Royal Albert Hall

The Royal Albert Hall was built in an Italian Renaissance style in 1867–71 to accommodate over 8000 people. The frieze outside illustrates the triumph of the arts. It is most famous for its Promenade Concerts. The 'Proms' were created in 1895 by conductor Sir Henry Wood at the Queen's Hall, Langham Place. The Proms are now given at the Royal Albert Hall every weekday between mid-July and mid-September, culminating in the famous 'Last Night of the Proms'.

Wigmore Hall

Wigmore Hall is the perfect environment for recitals, chamber music and concerts. It is a home to regular performances of outstanding singers of the day and small musical ensembles. The atmosphere, the comfortable seating and the near–perfect acoustics create the ideal setting for intimate concerts. It is especially well known for its Sunday morning concerts, which include coffee and sherry.

London Coliseum

The London Coliseum is the home of the English National Opera. The operas here are presented in English and the company has a reputation for producing dazzling performances which often border on the *avant garde*.

London Villains

London villains

London has always had a strange affection for villains and since the Middle Ages it has been the home of an almost endless list of criminals. The real ones range from Richard Pudlicott, who stole the treasures of Westminster Abbey in 1303; Elizabeth Brownrigg, a midwife who imprisoned and tortured numerous young girls and was eventually hanged in 1767; to near-contemporary villains like the great train robbers and the Kray brothers. The fictional list includes Shakespeare's gang based at the Boar's Head in Eastcheap, John Gay's sexy highwayman

Elizabeth Brownrigg

Macheath (*The Beggar's Opera,* first performed in 1728), Dickens' thief-runner Fagin and murderer Bill Sykes (*Oliver Twist* 1837–39), Conan Doyle's criminal mastermind Moriarty, Sapper's genius of disguise Carl Peterson, and George Macdonald Fraser's cad Flashman (borrowed from Thomas Hughes).

Cutpurses and pickpockets

In 1581 Wootton, a once successful merchant who fell on hard times, kept an alehouse near Billingsgate. According to a pamphlet of the time: 'He procured all the cutpurses about this city to repair to his said house. There was a schoolhouse set up to learn young boys to cut purses. There were hung up two devices, the one was a pocket, the other was a purse. The pocket had in it certain counters, and was hung about with bells and he that could take out a counter without any noise was allowed to be a public pickpocket, and he that could take a piece of silver out of the purse without the noise of any of the bells, he was adjudged a pickpurse or cutpurse.'

NOTES

Highwaymen

The famous highwayman Claude Duval was noted for
prowling the Hornsey Road area, formerly Devil's Lane. Once
he stopped a lady's coach in which there was £400, and
returned the woman £300 in exchange for a dance with her.
Duval was caught while drunk, and hanged in 1670. His body
lay in state in a tavern before being buried by torchlight in St
Paul's, Covent Garden, where a stone proclaims:

> Here lies Du Vall: Reader, if male thou art
> Look to thy purse; if female to thy heart.

In 1749 Horace Walpole (1717–97), the author of Gothic
novels, was robbed by the fashionable highwayman James
Maclean. He described the incident in his diary: 'One night,
in the beginning of November, as I was returning from
Holland House by moonlight, about 10 o'clock, I was
attacked by two highwaymen in Hyde Park, and the pistol of
one of them going off accidentally, razed the skin under my
eye, left some marks of shot on my face, and stunned me.'
The next year Maclean, a former grocer and the son of an
Irish dean, was caught and hanged at Tyburn. Many ladies of
high birth were said to have wept inconsolably at his death.

Jack the Ripper

The most famous murderer in the history of London was Jack the Ripper. Between August and November 1888 at least six, and perhaps as many as 13, prostitutes were murdered and mutilated by him in London's East End. The name was one he gave himself in a note he sent to the press: 'I am down on whores and I shan't quit ripping them till I do get buckled. Grand work the last job was. I gave the lady no time to squeal. How can they catch me now? I love my work and want to start again …' A second postcard, marked with a bloody thumbprint, arrived on 30 September: 'You'll hear about Saucy Jack's work tomorrow. Double event this time. Number One squealed a bit. Couldn't finish straight off. Had no time to get ears for police.' No one ever proved who Jack the Ripper was, and suspects have included leading politicians of the time and members of the royal family.

FINANCIAL LONDON

Financial London

For three centuries London has been one of the most important financial centres in the world. The foundation of the Bank of England, together with the growth of trade in stocks and shares, provided England with the basis for a true capitalist economy, while Lloyd's of London became the dominant power in the worldwide insurance market. The first purpose-built stock exchange was built in London in 1773. During the 19th century the London Stock Exchange was undoubtedly the most important in the world. It lost pride of place to Wall Street at the beginning of the 20th century, but remains the third most important after New York and Tokyo. During the late 1980s, prompted by mergers and deregulation (the so-called Big Bang) London's financial markets grew explosively, though the recession of the early 1990s put on a sharp brake.

Lloyd's of London

Lloyd's of London has long been the most famous insurance name in the world. It started in a coffee house frequented by shipowners and underwriters who met to arrange insurance contracts during the 1680s. The present building in Lime Street, designed by Richard Rogers, dates from 1986. This high-tech building, with external piping, should be seen at night when floodlighting illuminates its unusual features.

The Bank of England

The Bank of England was founded in 1694, and nationalised in 1946. It acts as banker to the government and other British banks, issues notes, and manages the National Debt. Under the ultimate control of the government, it sets the bank rate, which influences the general level of interest rates throughout Britain. The Governor of the Bank of England is appointed by the Prime Minister, and is second only to the Chancellor of the Exchequer as a maker of economic policy.

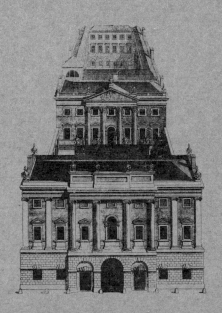

NOTES

POLITICAL LONDON

HOME RULE BILL

Political London

London has been the political capital of England for a thousand years or more, and the Anglo-Saxon forerunner of Parliament, the Witan, met here. In the 13th century Parliaments began regularly to meet in London, and the establishment of parliamentary control over taxation during the long wars with France was crucial to the development of England's democratic tradition. After the Act of Union with Scotland in 1707, London became the capital of Britain. Because of London's long-standing dominance of the nation, a recent political history of Great Britain is virtually interchangeable with the political history of London, though the city also has its own local government traditions.

Elizabeth I was the last ruler to live in the country and every monarch since has lived in or close by London. George II (r.1727–1760) loaned 10 Downing Street to the first Prime Minister, Sir Robert Walpole.

It may be here observed that the political consequence of the British senate is not attended with that parade and solemnity which create respect and inspire confidence. Members reclining on benches, equipped with hats and boots, seem ... prepared to dispute upon the laws of the turf, than to enter into a serious debate concerning the state of the nation.

The Gentleman's Magazine, 1799

NOTES

The Houses of Parliament

Five months after the fire of 1834 which destroyed the Houses of Parliament, a committee agreed that the buildings should be rebuilt in Tudor or Gothic style, to blend with the surviving medieval buildings. A national competition was held, and the winner out of 97 suggested designs was by Charles Barry. The foundation stone was laid in April 1840 and the House of Commons finally took its place in 1852, five years after the House of Lords. The new Houses of Parliament cost two million pounds to build. They have 1100 rooms, 100 staircases, 11 courtyards, and 2 miles of passages. The elaborate detail of the building, including even the furniture and fittings, were personally designed by Barry's collaborator Augustus Pugin. Electric lighting was installed in the Lords chamber in 1883, but not in the Commons until 1912. Similarly, the proceedings of the House of Lords were televised several years before those of the Commons.

Downing Street

10 Downing Street has been the official residence of the British Prime Minister since 1732. Numbers 11 and 12, the official residences of the Chancellor of the Exchequer and the Chief Whip, are also original late 17th-century buildings. During riots in the early 1830s a mob ran into Downing Street and rushed up to the guard at the door shouting, 'Liberty or death!' The soldier raised his gun and replied, 'Hands off, you fellows! I know nothing about liberty; but if you come a step further, I'll show you what death is!' Since 1989 there has been a security gate across the entrance of the street, though the IRA still managed to fire a mortar shell into the garden of Number 10.

NOTES

Sights of
London

MUSEUMS &
GALLERIES

*I*n the 17th century London offered the intrepid
visitor and the well-connected Londoner several places
to satisfy the burgeoning curiosity that was typical of the age.
In the Lambeth physic garden which occupied a site in the
church grounds of St Mary-at-Lambeth, a visitor could
peruse, in a leisurely fashion, rare plants, beasts, fishes,
worms, precious stones, coins, shells, feathers and also various
curiosities of carving and painting. The collection formed the
basis of Oxford's Ashmolean Museum. The **Museum of
Garden History** now stands on the site of the original
garden. In the **Tower of London**, another popular sight of
the period, a one and a half yard long unicorn's horn worth at
the time twenty thousand pounds sterling attracted many
bewildered visitors. At Sir Henry Moody's in the Strand the
public could view an image projected into a camera obscura.
Although there were some galleries in Georgian London, such
as the **National Gallery**, major museum building was left to
the Victorians.

NOTES

The British Museum

The British Museum houses the most extensive collection of
antiquities in the world. It was built between 1823 and 1847,
and is based on Sir Hans Sloane's collection, which had been
shown in public since 1759. Among its most famous exhibits
are the Rosetta Stone, a collection of Assyrian winged bulls,

Egyptian mummies and sculptures and friezes from the Parthenon. There are sculptures from the tomb of Mausolus, one of the destroyed Seven Wonders of the World; a wide assortment of Chinese and Indian work; Michelangelo's cartoon *Epifania;* the Magna Carta; the Gutenberg Bible; and treasures from Anglo-Saxon ship burials. The Reading Room is where Karl Marx wrote *Das Kapital.*

> Stone lies solid over the British Museum, as bone
> lies cool over visions and heat of the brain. Only
> here the brain is Plato's brain and Shakespeare's;
> the brain has made pots and statues, great bulls
> and little jewels ...
>
> Virginia Woolf, *Jacob's Room,* 1922

The Tate Gallery

The Tate Gallery, Millbank, opened in 1897 on the site of a
converted prison, contains a collection of English painting
from 1500, together with an international modern collection
which includes works by Cézanne, Van Gogh, a beautiful
clothed wax model of a young dancer by Degas and an
impressive collection of sculptures and paintings by Giacometti.
More recent styles are represented by rooms devoted to Abstract
Impressionism and today's *avant garde*. The mood changes
when the visitor enters the **Clore Gallery**, devoted to the
career of Turner from his early topographic drawings through
to the intense colour compositions of his later years. The Tate
also has a incomparable collection of pre-Raphaelite paintings.

The National Portrait Gallery

This ever-popular gallery was founded in 1856 to represent 'a
gallery of the Portraits of the most Eminent Persons in British
history'. From the Tudor period there are portraits of Elizabeth I
and Shakespeare. A wonderful miniature of Oliver Cromwell is
among the 17th century portraits, while the fascinating Georgian
collection includes the only known portrait of Jane Austen and a
self–portrait by William Hogarth. There is a splendid portrait of
the romantic Robert Burns, and the Brontë sisters are among
the luminaries represented in the Victorian rooms. The ground
floor is jam-packed with notable faces from this century.

Madame Tussaud's

One of London's most popular sights began life as an exhibition in Paris about 1780. Madame Tussaud was a celebrity who knew everyone from King Louis XVI to Voltaire. In 1802 she began to travel around Britain with her show, but the ship carrying her to Ireland sank with all her waxworks. However, she started again, and in 1833 settled the exhibition in Baker Street. The famous Chamber of Horrors was very popular with the Duke of Wellington, but *Punch* magazine compared Madame Tussaud with witches who made wax images of those they wished to destroy.

The National Gallery

The National Gallery was founded in 1824 to display a collection of 38 Old Master paintings that the government had bought. The main building itself was opened in 1838. As one of the leading art galleries in the world, a list of its world-famous paintings would last several pages. These are just a few highlights: *The Wilton Diptych*; Botticelli's *Venus and Mars*; Leonardo da Vinci's *Cartoon of the Virgin and Child*; Holbein's *The Ambassadors*; Titian's *Bacchus and Ariadne*; Van Eyck's *The Arnolfini Marriage*; Rembrandt's *Self-Portrait*; Rubens' *Samson and Delilah*; Turner's *The Fighting Téméraire*; Constable's *The Haywain*; Velásquez's *Rokeby Venus*; Seurat's *The Bathers*; and Van Gogh's *Sunflowers*.

231

The Science Museum

This museum is not to be missed, with its marvellous exhibits devoted to discoveries, inventions and models, many of which are interactive learning experiences. There are five floors filled with such diverse items as steam engines, computers, rocket pods, motor bikes, old printing presses and holograms.

Natural History Museum

The natural history department of the British Museum was moved to the Natural History Museum when it opened in 1880, having been built on a site bought with the profits of the Great Exhibition. Among the most popular exhibits are a full-size model of a blue whale, a permanent exhibition on ecology, another on insects, and a moving dinosaur panorama. There are cases of stuffed animals, birds and reptiles from all over the world.

The Victoria and Albert Museum

The V&A, as it is known, grew from the Great Exhibition of 1851, and was established in Cromwell Road in 1857 'to assemble a splendid collection of objects representing the application of fine art to manufactures'. It was given its present name in 1899. It contains an unparalleled collection of English furniture, as well as proving, in the words of a former director, 'an extremely capacious handbag' with exhibits ranging from sculptures by Rodin to Elizabethan miniatures by Nicholas Hilliard, the Great Bed of Ware, cartoons by Raphael, casts of some of the greatest sculptures from the Italian Renaissance, fashion through the ages, the William Morris room, and special galleries devoted to a diverse range of cultures. It is a wonderful place in which to get lost for a day, with its galleries and staircases leading the visitor deeper into its almost unfathomable interior full of surprising discoveries.

Sir John Soane's Museum

One of the architects who helped Nash transform the face of London was Sir John Soane, known primarily as the architect of the original Bank of England, and an avid collector of antiquities. Soane was an inveterate collector and filled his house at 13 Lincoln's Inn Fields with curiosities. In 1833 he obtained an Act of Parliament to preserve his museum, library and works of art 'for the benefit of the public, and for establishing a sufficient endowment for the due maintenance of the same'. The Sir John Soane's Museum opened in 1837; the house is still almost exactly as Soane left it.

The Museum of London

This marvellous museum traces the social history of London and Londoners from Londinium, as it was called in 34BC, to the 20th century. Featuring such diverse displays as the remains of the Temple of Mithras, 11th century Norman battle axes, the arms and costumes worn by the great Tudors, the death mask of Oliver Cromwell, a mind-boggling diorama of the Great Fire complete with sound effects, the reconstruction of an Edwardian street and pub and a 1928 elevator from **Selfridges**, this museum is a must for any visitor with the slightest curiosity about London.

The Royal Academy of Arts

The Royal Academy of Arts was founded in 1768 and included Constable and Turner as early pupils. Since 1868 it has been housed at **Burlington House**. Enlarged in 1874, and most recently in 1991, when the Sackler Galleries were added, there are now 17 main galleries, a library, members rooms and studios for the Art School.

Every year the famous Summer Exhibition takes place and the Academy regularly hosts important international loan exhibitions, thus contributing to London's continuing prominence in the contemporary art world.

Parks and Gardens

*T*he parks of London were described by politician William Pitt the Elder in the 18th century as the 'lungs of London'. As a result of land appropriations by Royalty throughout the past 500 years, London's parks have remained oases of water and greenery for Londoners and visitors alike.

When the monasteries were dissolved by Henry VIII, **Hyde Park**, which used to belong to the monks of Westminster Abbey, was used by Henry and later opened to the people. Likewise **Green Park**, **St James's Park**, **Richmond Park** and later **Regent's Park** were transformed from hunting grounds of the monarchs to landscaped spaces for the public.

Two parks were created specifically for Londoners living in crowded conditions around the city – **Victoria Park** and **Finsbury Park**. George Bernard Shaw describes Victoria Park in *Candida* (1897): 'a lake for bathers, flower beds which are the triumphs of the admired cockney art of carpet gardening'.

Hyde Park

I was to be found every season of the year in Hyde Park because that was where I learnt my English. As a foreigner, I enjoyed ideas and every idea was thrashed out in the Park. You could learn more by mixing with the riff-raff at Marble Arch in one hour than by a thousand walks from Hyde Park Corner to Albert Gate in the season. Besides you could take your lectures lying down at Marble Arch. The greensward is the natural couch of man and the people for whose sake you had to avoid everything that was natural were not to be seen.

George Bernard Shaw, letter to Stephen Winston, late 19th century

St James's Park

If a man be splenetic, he may every day meet companions on the seats in St James's Park, with whose groans he may mix his own, and pathetically talk of the weather.

Oliver Goldsmith (1730-74)

Regent's Park

Mrs Vanelden's house was situated in one of the moon-coloured Crescents, or Circuses, bordering on the edge of Regent's Park. Two Crescents, one on either side, overlooked large gardens full of huge purring leaves and great bright flowers, pale yellow begonias that made you think of South America because of their Creole complexions; and here, shrouded by the great leaves of the trees and bushes, the young people played tennis; from the windows of the houses, or if you sat beneath the awnings that sheltered the balconies, you could hear their voices calling each other, although you could not see them, you could only, at moments, see a white dress, a glint of gold or bird-dark, bird-glossy hair as they passed among the trees.

Edith Sitwell, *I Live under a Black Sun*, 1937

Hampstead Heath

In Hampstead Heath you will find beauty in all seasons. The undulating country is so full of variation that you find nearly all the artistic effects that European painters have depicted.

Steen Eiler Rasmussen,
London: The Unique City, 1937

Notes

The Royal Botanic Gardens, Kew

Kew Gardens, largely the creation of George III and the famous landscape gardener Capability Brown, have belonged to the nation since 1840. Within the gardens there are three glasshouses, each full of exotic plants and trees, as well as the Chinese Pogoda that enhances the feeling of romance and timelessness a visit to Kew evokes. Darwin praised them:

> So sits enthron'd in vegetable pride
> Imperial Kew, by Thames's glittering side.

SHOPPING

As long ago as 1498 an Italian visitor commented on the astonishing richness of London's shops. **Regent Street** houses a bevy of wonderful shops including **Dickens and Jones, Liberty** and **Hamleys** (toys), while **Oxford Street** is over a mile in length and contains **Selfridges,** London's first real department store, **Marks and Spencer, Debenhams, British Home Stores, House of Fraser** stores and **John Lewis. Bond Street** has designer clothes shops and jewellers. **Piccadilly, Savile Row, St James's** and **Jermyn Street** contain famous and long-established shops such as **Hatchard's** (books), **Swaine Adney Brigg** (umbrellas, hunting gear and luggage), **Simpson's** (clothing), **Fortnum and Mason** (food), **Lobb** (shoes) and **Lock and Co** (hats). **Knightsbridge** is another leading shopping area, with **Harrods** and **Harvey Nichols.** Further along the **King's Road,** Chelsea, are a variety of antique and designer clothes shops.

FINAL THOUGHTS

Sights

Albert Memorial, South Carriage Drive, Kensington
   Gardens, SW7

Bank of England, Threadneedle Street, EC2

Banqueting House, Whitehall, SW1

Buckingham Palace, The Mall, SW1

Chelsea Royal Hospital, Royal Hospital Road, SW3

Cleopatra's Needle, Embankment, WC2

Downing Street, SW1

George Inn, 77 Borough High Street, SE1

Greenwich Palace and Royal Naval College, Park Row, SE10

Guildhall, Aldermanbury, EC2

Hampton Court Palace, East Molesey, Surrey

Highgate Cemetery, Swain's Lane, N6

Horse Guards, Whitehall, SW1

Houses of Parliament, Westminster, SE1

Inns of Court, Lincoln's Inn Fields, Holborn, WC2

Kensington Palace, Palace Avenue, W8

Lambeth Palace, Lambeth Palace Road, SE1

London Zoo, Regent's Park, NW1

Mansion House, Walbrook, EC4

Monument, Monument Street, EC3

Nelson's Column, Trafalgar Square, WC2

Old Royal Observatory, Greenwich Park, SE10

Piccadilly Circus, W1

Prospect of Whitby, 57 Wapping Wall, E1

Royal Courts of Justice (Old Bailey), Strand, WC2

Savoy Hotel, Strand, WC2

Staple Inn, Holborn, WC1

St James's Palace, The Mall, SW1

St Katharine's Dock, E1

Tower Bridge, Tower Bridge Approach, SE1

Tower of London, Tower Hill, EC3

Trafalgar Square, WC2

Wellington Arch, Hyde Park Corner, SW1

Westminster Hall (Palace of Westminster), SW1

Ye Olde Cheshire Cheese, 145 Fleet Street, EC4

Churches

Chelsea Old Church, Cheyne Walk, SW3

Christ Church, Spitalfields, Commercial Street, E1

The Oratory, Brompton Road, SW7

St Bride's, Fleet Street, EC4

St James's, 197 Piccadilly, W1

St John's, Waterloo Road, SE1

St Martin-in-the-Fields, Trafalgar Square, WC2

St Mary-le-Bow, Cheapside, EC2

St Paul's Cathedral, Ludgate Hill, EC4

Southwark Cathedral, Montague Close, SE1

Westminster Abbey, Broad Sanctuary, SW1

Museums

Apsley House, 149 Piccadilly, W1

Bethnal Green Museum of Childhood, Cambridge Heath
 Road, E2

British Museum and Library, Great Russell Street, WC1

Chiswick House, Burlington Lane, W4

Courtauld Institute Galleries, Somerset House, Strand, WC2

Design Museum, Shad Thames, SE1

Dickens' House, 48 Doughty Street, WC1

Dulwich Picture Gallery, College Road, SE21

Geffrye Museum, Kingsland Road, E2

Geological Museum, Exhibition Road, SW7

Hayward Gallery, South Bank Centre, SE1

Imperial War Museum, Lambeth Road, SE1

Keats House, Keats Grove, Hampstead, NW3

Kenwood House, Hampstead Lane, NW3

Leighton House, 12 Holland Park Road, W14

London Dungeon, Tooley Street, SE1

London Toy and Model Museum, 21–23 Craven Hill, W2

London Transport Museum, Covent Garden, WC2

Madame Tussaud's, Marylebone Road, NW1

Museum of London, London Wall, EC2

Museum of Mankind, 6 Burlington Gardens, W1

Museum of the Moving Image, and National Film Theatre,
 South Bank Arts Centre, SE1

National Army Museum, Royal Hospital Road, Chelsea, SW3
National Gallery, Trafalgar Square, WC2
National Maritime Museum, Greenwich, SE10
National Portrait Gallery, 2 St Martin's Place, WC2
Natural History Museum, Cromwell Road, SW7
Planetarium, Marylebone Road, NW1
Queen's Gallery, Buckingham Palace Road, SW1
Royal Academy of Arts, Burlington House, Piccadilly, W1
Science Museum, Exhibition Road, SW7
Sir John Soane's Museum, 13 Lincoln's Inn Fields, WC2
Tate Gallery, Millbank, SW1
Theatre Museum, 7 Russell Street, Covent Garden, WC2
Victoria and Albert Museum, Cromwell Road, SE7
Wallace Collection, Hertford House, Manchester Square, W1
Whitechapel Art Gallery, Whitechapel High St, E1

Theatres, Concert Halls and Opera Houses

Adelphi Theatre, Strand, WC2

Aldwych Theatre, Aldwych, WC2

Apollo Theatre, Shaftesbury Avenue, W1

Barbican Theatre (Royal Shakespeare Company) and Concert Hall, Silk Street, Barbican, EC2

Coliseum (English National Opera), St Martin's Lane, WC2

Criterion, Piccadilly Circus, W1

Duke of York's, St Martin's Lane, WC2

Gielgud Theatre, Shaftesbury Avenue, W1

Globe Theatre, Bankside, SE1

Lyric Theatre, Shaftesbury Avenue, W1

Mayfair Theatre, Stratton Street, W1

Mermaid Theatre, Puddle Dock, EC4

Old Vic, Waterloo Road, SE1

Open Air Theatre, Regent's Park, NW1

Palladium, Argyll Street, W1

Prince of Wales Theatre, Coventry Street, W1

Purcell Rooms, South Bank Centre, SE1

Queen Elizabeth Hall, South Bank Centre, SE1

Riverside Studios, Crisp Road, Hammersmith, W6

Royal Albert Hall, Kensington Gore, SW7

Royal Court Theatre, Sloane Square, SW1

Royal Festival Hall, South Bank Centre, SE1

Royal National Theatre, South Bank Centre, SE1

Royal Opera House, Floral Street, Covent Garden, WC2
Strand Theatre, Aldwych, WC2
Theatre Royal, Drury Lane, WC2
Theatre Royal, Haymarket, SW1
Tricycle Theatre, Kilburn High Road, NW6
Wembley Arena, Empire Way, Wembley
Wigmore Hall, 36 Wigmore Street, W1
Whitehall Theatre, Whitehall, SW1
Wyndham's Theatre, Charing Cross Road, WC2
Young Vic, The Cut, Waterloo Road, SE1

Parks and Gardens
Battersea Park, Albert Bridge Road, SW8
Chelsea Physic Garden, Swan Walk, SW3
Green Park, Constitution Hill, SW1
Hampstead Heath, Heath Road, NW3
Holland Park, Abbotsbury Road, W14
Hyde Park, Park Lane, W2
Kensington Gardens, Kensington Road, W8
Kew Gardens (Royal Botanic Gardens), Richmond
Regent's Park, NW1
Richmond Park, Richmond
St James's Park, SW1
Syon Park, London Road, Brentford

Markets

Bermondsey Market, Bermondsey Street, SE1

Brick Lane, E1

Camden Lock, off Chalk Farm Road, NW1

Camden Passage, off Upper Street, Islington, N1

Chapel Market, Islington, N1

Covent Garden, WC2

Kensington Church Street, W8

Leather Lane, EC1

Petticoat Lane Market, off Middlesex Street, E1

Portobello Road, W11

Smithfield Market, Charterhouse Street, EC1

Spitalfields, EC2

Shopping

Brompton Road, Knightsbridge, SW3

Carnaby Street, off Marlborough Street, W1

Charing Cross Road, WC2

Covent Garden, WC2

King's Road, Chelsea, SW1

New and Old Bond Street, W1

Oxford Street, W1

Regent Street, SW1

South Molton Street, W1

St Christopher's Place, W1

Architecture

The Ark, Hammersmith
Canada Tower, Canary Wharf, E14
Lloyd's Building, 1 Lime Street, EC3
St Pancras Station, Euston Road, NW1
Tower Bridge, SE1
Westminster Bridge, SW1

Squares

Bloomsbury Square, WC1
Bedford Square, WC1
Berkeley Square, W1
Brunswick Square, WC1
Cavendish Square, W1
Fitzroy Square, W1
Great Cumberland Place, W1
Hanover Square, W1
Soho Square, W1

Museum Quilts would like to thank the following people whose assistance contributed to the preparation of this book.

Judy Gordon

Notions Antiquaria, 24 Cecil Court, Charing Cross Road, London WC2.

Tracy Brett, 174 Oldfield Grove, London SE16.

Michael Finney, Antique Books and Prints, 11 Camden Passage, Islington, London N1.

Published by Passport Books
a division of NTC/Contemporary Publishing Company
4255 West Touhy Avenue
Lincolnwood (Chicago), Illinois 60646–1975, U.S.A.
© 1997 by Museum Quilts Publications, Inc.

ISBN: 0-8442-4891-6

First published in the United Kingdom by
Museum Quilts (UK) Inc.
254–258 Goswell Road
London EC1V 7EB

Printed and bound in Spain